Creating Safe Spaces and Finding Silver Linings During the Trump Presidency: A Guide to Resilience

Tumaini Rustin

Table of Contents

- o Benefits of Exercise, Journaling, and Art Therapy (e.g., Coloring Books)
- o Creating Joy with Pets and Fun Naming Ideas (e.g., "Harris" or "Obama")

13. **Volunteering for Causes That Matter**
   - o Opportunities in Anti-Racism, LGBT+ Support, Immigration Advocacy, and More
   - o How Volunteering Can Shift Focus and Uplift Communities

14. **Peaceful Activism and Community Involvement**
   - o Finding Peaceful Means to Express Your Voice
   - o Connecting with Like-Minded People and Local Organizations

15. **Building a Support Network for Difficult Times**
   - o The Value of Support from Friends, Family, and Online Communities
   - o Finding Local and National Support Groups

16. **Seeking Support from Health Professionals**
   - o How Medical and Mental Health Professionals Can Help
   - o When to Reach Out for Guidance and Understanding

17. **Embracing Peacefulness and Nonviolence**
   - o Finding Strength in Peaceful Responses
   - o How Peaceful Actions Reflect Your Personal Strength

18. **Why Self-Care and Community Support Help Manage Stress**
   - o Understanding the Impact of Self-Care on Long-Term Wellness
   - o The Power of Helping Others to Build Your Own Resilience

Chapter 1: Introduction to Resilience in Challenging Times

In times of political change, especially when a leader with polarizing policies takes office, it's natural to feel a range of emotions—from fear and anger to anxiety and confusion. If you're feeling any of these emotions after Donald Trump's election victory, know that you're not alone. Many people across the country are processing similar feelings, wondering what these next four years will bring and how best to protect their peace of mind.

This guide is here to help you find resilience, even when the future feels uncertain. Resilience doesn't mean ignoring reality or forcing yourself to feel positive when you don't. Instead, resilience is about acknowledging what's difficult and finding small but meaningful ways to respond. It's about choosing to see challenges with a balanced mindset and empowering yourself to find purpose and peace in your everyday life. In moments like these, focusing on what you *can* control—even if it's just your thoughts or routines—can create a strong foundation for emotional well-being.

The Importance of Perspective and Positivity

When faced with circumstances that feel beyond your control, maintaining perspective can be one of the most effective ways to cope. Perspective doesn't deny the challenges in front of us; it's a way to keep them in context. Consider that while a president's policies may impact broad aspects of society, many of your daily actions, values, and personal choices remain under your control. Your resilience will come from remembering that you have the power to adapt and to create a positive space for yourself, even in difficult times.

Positivity isn't about looking at everything through rose-colored glasses. It's about actively seeking moments of hope and small victories. By focusing on the silver linings, no matter how small, you can reduce stress and build confidence. For instance, if a policy change disrupts your expectations, look for any positive outcomes or new possibilities. This shift in mindset might not alter the policy, but it will help you feel more in control of your reaction.

Finding the Silver Lining

Each major policy shift in the Trump administration will be explored in the coming chapters. After breaking down each policy, we'll find the "silver lining"—a way to reframe the policy that provides a source of hope, opportunity, or even constructive action. It may be challenging, but each silver lining you find builds a sense of strength and optimism. This can be your personal tool for managing stress and finding meaning, even when a policy doesn't align with your beliefs.

For example, if immigration policies change in ways that feel restrictive, this might prompt a surge of interest in local immigration advocacy groups. By reframing a policy as an opportunity to connect with supportive organizations, you can feel empowered and take concrete actions that align with your values.

The Role of Personal Choices in Creating Peace

Remember, no matter who sits in the Oval Office, you still have the power to make choices that contribute to your well-being. You decide the people you surround yourself with, the news you consume, and the causes you support. By making thoughtful choices, you create a safe space that reflects your values and promotes a healthy mind.

To prepare for the next chapters, take a moment to list a few core values that matter to you—whether they include kindness, equality, or growth. When political news feels overwhelming, let these values remind you of what you stand for. They'll act as your compass, guiding you as you move forward and helping you filter through the noise.

What It Means to "Find the Silver Lining"

Throughout this guide, you'll encounter the term "silver lining." Silver linings are a reminder that, while the situation may seem bleak, there's still light to be found. Finding silver linings doesn't erase the challenges but brings balance by offering hope.

With each policy that may seem intimidating, this guide will help you find practical ways to reinterpret it, uncovering any benefits that might come out of difficult situations. Reframing is a powerful tool to build resilience and stay grounded. It helps shift your focus from anxiety to action, making you feel like you're not just weathering the storm, but using it to grow stronger.

As you move through each chapter, keep in mind that resilience is a journey. Some days will feel easy, and others will feel difficult. Take things one day at a time, and remember that every effort you make toward positivity and peace strengthens your ability to cope and thrive.

Chapter 2: Economic Policies — Finding Opportunity Amid Change

Economic policy changes can often feel overwhelming. Whether they involve tax reforms, adjustments to social safety nets, or job creation strategies, economic policies can impact our lives in very real ways. With Donald Trump's administration prioritizing certain economic shifts, it's natural to feel uncertain about how these changes may affect you. This chapter will break down some of the key aspects of these policies and guide you in identifying possible silver linings.

By choosing to see opportunities, even in situations that may feel difficult, you'll be able to cultivate a mindset that is both realistic and resilient. Each policy is a chance to learn something new about yourself, your community, and even your potential for growth.

Analyzing Policy: Job Creation and Tax Reforms

One of the central themes of Trump's economic agenda is a focus on job creation through tax cuts and deregulation. While his administration might claim that reducing corporate taxes will drive more companies to invest domestically, you may be worried about whether these policies will truly translate to more stable, quality jobs for the everyday person.

While it's common to feel anxious about the direction of tax reforms, consider the potential opportunities. A renewed emphasis on business growth can sometimes stimulate innovation, especially for those willing to think creatively. While large corporations may benefit from these changes, small business owners and entrepreneurs could also find new pathways to explore, whether by creating side businesses or by tapping into the freelance economy.

Silver Lining: Opportunities in Innovation and Entrepreneurship

When economic shifts happen, they often open new doors for those who are ready to adapt. With deregulation and a focus on economic expansion, there may be increased support for start-ups, online businesses, and freelance work. If you've been considering starting a business, expanding a creative project, or even freelancing part-time, now may be a great time to explore these options.

These policies could make it easier for you to access resources or funding that weren't as available before. Take advantage of online courses or business seminars to help you get started. Use this moment as motivation to pursue a dream or side project. In the long run, such steps not only benefit you financially but also give you a greater sense of control over your professional future.

Analyzing Policy: Cuts to Social Programs

Another potential shift in Trump's economic policy could involve reductions in certain social programs. For those who rely on these programs, changes can understandably be stressful. But remember that even if a policy creates initial uncertainty, it doesn't necessarily mean that you are without support or options. This can be an opportunity to explore other resources and to focus on building community connections that provide mutual aid and assistance.

Silver Lining: Empowering Personal Financial Resilience

While it may seem counterintuitive, periods of economic change often prompt people to become more proactive about their personal finances. Budgeting, saving, and looking for new ways to generate income can help you build financial resilience. Consider joining a local financial planning group or seeking advice from a trusted advisor who can help you navigate these changes.

If a social program you rely on is altered, explore community-based options for support. Many local organizations offer assistance, often more personally and directly than larger programs. Engaging with your community in this way can help reduce feelings of isolation and reinforce that you're not alone in adapting to new realities.

Analyzing Policy: Market Deregulation and Corporate Growth

Deregulation policies are often aimed at encouraging corporate investment and reducing operational costs for businesses. While this may lead to economic growth in certain sectors, you may be concerned about its impact on environmental standards, worker protections, or small businesses. This is where a shift in perspective can be useful, as it allows you to find benefits, even if the policy doesn't align with all of your values.

Silver Lining: Increased Advocacy for Ethical Businesses

When corporate growth becomes a priority, so does the power of the consumer voice. Now, more than ever, you have the ability to support companies and brands that align with your values. Many consumers are now drawn to businesses that are socially responsible, environmentally conscious, and worker-friendly. This increased demand can lead to a market that is more driven by consumer values.

Take this opportunity to become a more conscious consumer, supporting ethical businesses and companies with transparent practices. By spending thoughtfully, you're sending a message about the importance of responsible business practices. Additionally, community members who are passionate about ethical business can come together, share resources, and support each other in choosing companies that contribute positively to society.

Embracing Economic Resilience as a Tool for Self-Confidence

Economic policies may impact us, but they don't have to control us. Finding silver linings is a powerful way to retain a sense of agency and confidence. By choosing to see opportunity where others might see only limitations, you cultivate a mindset that is both adaptable and empowered.

Remember, your ability to adapt to economic changes strengthens your resilience. Use these shifts as a chance to learn, grow, and perhaps even explore new financial pathways. Not only will this reduce stress, but it will also give you the assurance that you can thrive, regardless of the political climate.

4o

Chapter 3: Healthcare Policies — Focusing on Personal Health and Community Support

Changes to healthcare policy are often one of the most sensitive topics, as they can affect everything from insurance coverage to access to medications and mental health resources. Donald Trump's administration has signaled potential changes in healthcare that could involve restructuring insurance plans, adjusting coverage for pre-existing conditions, and introducing new healthcare models. For many, these policy shifts create feelings of uncertainty about the accessibility and affordability of necessary healthcare.

In times like these, focusing on personal health practices, self-advocacy, and community-based support can help you stay resilient, informed, and empowered. This chapter will provide an analysis of some anticipated changes in healthcare policy and suggest constructive ways to respond by prioritizing your well-being.

Analyzing Policy: Insurance and Coverage Changes

One of the most significant concerns regarding Trump's healthcare policies is the potential for adjustments to insurance structures, including coverage for pre-existing conditions. Changes in policy could lead to variations in what is covered, creating new out-of-pocket expenses for certain treatments or medications. For individuals managing chronic conditions, this can understandably cause worry.

Silver Lining: Empowering Personal Health Awareness

If you find yourself facing changes in healthcare coverage, one positive step you can take is to strengthen your knowledge of personal health management. Focus on preventive care and wellness habits that support your body and mind, potentially reducing your need for frequent medical care.

Taking small steps toward physical health, like incorporating regular exercise, balanced nutrition, and stress management practices, can have a major impact on your overall wellness. By prioritizing these areas, you gain more control over your health and can potentially lower your need for extensive medical care. For example, activities like walking, yoga, or even light stretching can reduce stress and improve physical resilience.

Additionally, exploring local resources like community health centers, sliding-scale clinics, or telehealth options can provide affordable ways to access healthcare services. Look into community-driven healthcare programs that may offer assistance, and be proactive in finding support through these alternatives.

Analyzing Policy: Mental Health Support Accessibility

Healthcare policy changes can also affect mental health resources, including counseling services and psychiatric care. Adjustments to insurance coverage or funding for mental health programs might make access to these services more challenging, but there are silver linings that can still provide ways to find support.

Silver Lining: Building Resilience through Community and Self-Care

If traditional access to mental health support becomes limited, consider alternative ways to maintain emotional well-being. Building a support network of friends, family, and like-minded people can help create a valuable outlet for discussing and processing your emotions. Peer support groups and community mental health organizations often offer free or low-cost counseling services, creating options for connection and encouragement during challenging times.

Embrace self-care practices that help you manage stress and support mental resilience. Activities like journaling, meditation, or even spending time in nature can all positively impact mental health. Remember, self-care doesn't have to be costly to be effective—it's about setting aside time to rest and recharge in ways that feel meaningful to you.

At the same time, mental health apps and online platforms can be great tools to explore affordable therapy options. Many of these digital services have sliding scales or offer free resources, such as guided meditations or mood trackers, to help you manage your mental well-being on a daily basis.

Analyzing Policy: Adjustments in Prescription Coverage

Changes in healthcare policy may also lead to adjustments in prescription coverage, possibly affecting the affordability and accessibility of medications. For those who rely on medications for chronic health conditions, these shifts can be a source of concern.

Silver Lining: Exploring Alternatives and Advocacy

If policy changes impact your ability to access certain medications, take time to explore alternatives. Talk with your doctor about generic or alternative medications, which may be more affordable while providing similar health benefits. Additionally, some pharmaceutical companies and non-profit organizations offer discount programs or financial assistance for essential medications. By researching these options, you can continue managing your health effectively, even if insurance policies shift.

Another proactive approach is to become involved in advocacy for healthcare reform. By volunteering with organizations that focus on healthcare rights or affordable access to medication, you can contribute to positive change. Supporting causes that align with your values allows you to engage constructively with the issue, build community, and push for improvements in healthcare policy.

Embracing Personal Health as a Path to Resilience

Healthcare policies may change, but your commitment to taking care of your health remains within your control. By focusing on preventive care, embracing wellness practices, and seeking community resources, you can manage healthcare shifts with a greater sense of confidence and calm. Personal health resilience doesn't mean that you're unaffected by policy changes—it means that you have strategies in place to support yourself, even during times of uncertainty.

In times of healthcare adjustments, knowledge and preparation are empowering. Take these opportunities to strengthen your understanding of health resources, both local and national, and to connect with people who share your concerns. Together, you can navigate policy shifts, advocate for change, and ensure that your health remains a priority.

Chapter 4: Immigration Policies — Supporting Diversity and Community Connection

Immigration policy changes are often deeply impactful, not only for individuals directly affected but also for communities as a whole. Under Donald Trump's administration, there may be increased emphasis on tightening immigration controls, stricter border enforcement, and potential changes to pathways for citizenship. For many, these shifts can create uncertainty, fear, and a sense of instability, especially for immigrant communities and their allies.

However, even in times of policy change, there are ways to find silver linings and opportunities to strengthen your commitment to diversity and inclusivity. By focusing on community involvement, advocacy, and supporting immigrant rights, you can contribute to a more welcoming environment for all. This chapter explores how to channel concerns into positive actions that build community and foster inclusivity.

Analyzing Policy: Stricter Border Enforcement and Immigration Controls

A major focus of Trump's immigration policy may include stricter border enforcement and new measures that limit the number of people able to enter the U.S. legally. While this may impact immigration flows and the experiences of newcomers, it also has the potential to spark greater community awareness and support for immigrant rights.

For those who feel that tighter restrictions compromise the country's diversity and humanitarian values, finding positive ways to advocate for inclusive policies can create a sense of agency.

Silver Lining: Opportunities for Cultural Preservation and Advocacy

With heightened attention on immigration issues, there's a unique opportunity for individuals and communities to come together in support of diversity. Consider getting involved with local organizations that work directly with immigrant communities, such as language support centers, refugee assistance programs, or community-based cultural initiatives.

By learning about and supporting immigrant-led businesses, participating in cultural exchange programs, or volunteering with local advocacy groups, you're helping to create an environment where all backgrounds are valued. This also provides you with meaningful ways to connect with others, learn about different cultures, and celebrate the richness that diversity brings to your community.

Analyzing Policy: Changes to Pathways for Citizenship

Another potential aspect of Trump's immigration agenda may involve changing or limiting pathways to citizenship, potentially making it more difficult for certain groups to achieve residency or citizenship status. For many families and individuals, these changes can create significant stress and uncertainty about their futures in the United States.

Silver Lining: Strengthening Support Networks for Immigrant Families

While these policy changes may feel discouraging, you can make a difference by supporting initiatives that provide assistance and resources to immigrant families. Many local organizations, religious groups, and non-profits offer support for immigrants facing legal, financial, or emotional challenges. Volunteering with these organizations, or even just showing up to their events, helps you become part of a network that prioritizes compassion and unity.

Consider reaching out to immigrant support organizations to see how you can assist. This could involve volunteering your time, donating to their causes, or participating in events that raise awareness. Even small acts of support contribute to a stronger, more connected community and demonstrate a commitment to inclusion and respect for all backgrounds.

Analyzing Policy: Emphasis on National Identity and Reduced Diversity Initiatives

Policies that emphasize a more limited definition of "national identity" or deprioritize diversity initiatives may create a sense of exclusion for immigrant communities. However, this also presents an opportunity for individuals and organizations to step up in building inclusive spaces and promoting diversity.

Silver Lining: Building Inclusive Community Spaces

Even if diversity initiatives are reduced at the federal level, individuals and community groups can foster inclusive spaces locally. Start by creating small "safe spaces" in your own circles—this could mean supporting local immigrant-owned businesses, organizing cultural awareness events, or simply sharing stories that celebrate the multicultural fabric of society.

Joining or creating community spaces, clubs, or events centered around multicultural learning can be a powerful way to promote inclusivity. These spaces not only help immigrant communities feel more welcome, but they also foster mutual understanding and build bridges between different backgrounds.

By making efforts to engage with people from various cultures and experiences, you're not only expanding your worldview but also contributing to a community that respects and values everyone's unique heritage.

Embracing Diversity and Advocacy as Personal Empowerment

While immigration policies may change, the values you hold—compassion, inclusivity, and community—remain constant. By supporting immigrant communities, promoting cultural exchange, and standing up for diversity, you're creating a space that's grounded in empathy and mutual respect.

Taking these steps not only benefits others but also provides a sense of purpose and agency in difficult times. Whether through direct involvement in immigrant support networks, promoting diversity in your daily life, or simply being an ally, you're contributing to a more inclusive society.

Remember, your actions and choices have an impact. When you engage with immigrant communities and advocate for inclusivity, you're embodying the values that help create a stronger, more united world. You'll find that as you work to uplift others, you also build resilience, purpose, and connection in your own life.

Chapter 5: Environmental Policies — Finding Purpose in Grassroots Action

Environmental policy is often a deeply personal issue, as it affects the air we breathe, the water we drink, and the natural beauty we enjoy. Under Donald Trump's administration, there may be changes to environmental regulations, including a shift toward deregulation and potentially reduced emphasis on climate change initiatives. For those who care deeply about the environment, these changes may feel frustrating and concerning, especially when thinking about long-term sustainability and climate impacts.

However, even in times of policy setbacks, there are positive ways to respond. By taking personal and community-based action, you can make meaningful contributions to environmental protection and become part of a growing movement of individuals dedicated to sustainability. This chapter explores potential changes to environmental policies and suggests ways to turn your passion for the planet into positive, impactful action.

Analyzing Policy: Reduced Environmental Regulations

One potential direction of Trump's environmental policy may involve reducing federal regulations on businesses regarding pollution, emissions, and natural resource management. While the administration may argue that deregulation supports economic growth, it's natural to feel concerned about the potential impacts on air and water quality, as well as on wildlife and natural ecosystems.

Silver Lining: Empowering Local and Grassroots Environmental Activism

With potential cuts to federal oversight, there's an increased opportunity for grassroots movements to take center stage. Local environmental advocacy groups, conservation organizations, and eco-friendly businesses can step in to address these gaps and work to protect natural resources at the community level.

Consider joining or supporting local environmental groups that focus on the issues you care most about. These organizations often lead initiatives like river clean-ups, tree-planting events, recycling drives, and community gardens. Even small contributions of your time or resources can have a meaningful impact. By participating in these efforts, you're making a difference and building a community of people who share your commitment to the environment.

If you don't have an environmental group nearby, think about starting a small initiative with friends or family members. Simple actions, like organizing a monthly litter clean-up or hosting educational events on sustainable living, create ripple effects that inspire others to join in and make a difference.

Analyzing Policy: Reduced Emphasis on Climate Change Initiatives

With possible shifts away from climate change-focused policies, you may feel worried about the nation's commitment to addressing global warming and reducing carbon emissions. While this can feel disheartening, remember that meaningful climate action doesn't have to come solely from the top. Grassroots climate initiatives and personal lifestyle changes can play a powerful role in reducing carbon footprints and raising awareness.

Silver Lining: Personal Sustainability and Climate Advocacy

In the face of reduced climate initiatives, this is an opportunity to make your own personal commitment to sustainable living. Small changes, like reducing single-use plastics, conserving energy at home, and choosing eco-friendly transportation options, can all help lower your carbon footprint. When these changes are practiced consistently, they become part of a larger collective effort toward sustainability.

Additionally, becoming a climate advocate within your circle can have a positive impact. You can share information on climate issues, raise awareness, and encourage friends and family to make sustainable choices. By supporting local businesses that prioritize eco-friendly practices, advocating for green policies in your city or town, and speaking out about climate issues, you contribute to a culture of environmental responsibility.

Your voice is powerful, and by using it to educate and inspire others, you're helping to build a broader movement dedicated to protecting the planet.

Analyzing Policy: Public Lands and Resource Management

Changes in public land policy or increased resource extraction on protected lands may also be part of Trump's environmental approach. For many, public lands represent a connection to nature and a source of recreation and well-being, so any policies that impact these areas can feel personal and deeply unsettling.

Silver Lining: Supporting Conservation Efforts and Outdoor Engagement

If federal protections on public lands are scaled back, you can support conservation efforts by engaging with organizations dedicated to preserving these spaces. Groups like the National Parks Conservation Association, local land trusts, and environmental nonprofits often work to protect and restore public lands. Donations, volunteer work, or simply raising awareness about their efforts can make a real difference in preserving these natural areas for future generations.

Engaging with public lands directly—by hiking, camping, or volunteering with conservation efforts—also fosters a stronger connection to nature and reminds you of the importance of these spaces. The more you engage with nature, the more empowered you'll feel to protect it. Even as policy changes may impact public lands, your efforts in conservation and advocacy ensure that these natural spaces remain valued and protected within your community.

Embracing Environmental Advocacy as a Path to Purpose

Although policy changes can feel discouraging, they also open the door for passionate individuals to take meaningful action. Environmental challenges require a collective effort and by choosing to engage, you become a vital part of the solution. Your actions, no matter how small, contribute to a culture of sustainability and help inspire others to care for the planet.

Taking part in environmental advocacy can bring a deep sense of purpose and satisfaction, knowing that you're actively working to protect the Earth for yourself and future generations. You're also joining a movement of people dedicated to positive change, creating a sense of camaraderie and shared values.

Remember, the health of the planet is an issue that transcends politics. By committing to environmentally conscious actions, supporting conservation efforts, and fostering awareness in your community, you're strengthening your resilience and contributing to a world that values and protects nature.

Chapter 6: Education and Funding Policies — Creating Community-Led Learning Opportunities

Education is a cornerstone of personal and social development, providing the tools for growth, critical thinking, and opportunity. With Donald Trump's administration, potential changes to education policy might include shifts in funding, support for public education, and the role of private and charter schools. These changes could affect the resources available to schools, the diversity of educational options, and the accessibility of higher education.

For those who value accessible, high-quality education for all, these shifts may create concern. However, even in the face of potential challenges, there are silver linings that allow you to support and strengthen learning within your community. By focusing on local initiatives, community-led learning, and resources for students, you can contribute positively to educational resilience and accessibility.

Analyzing Policy: Shifts in Public Education Funding

One of the possible policy directions under Trump's administration is a shift in funding for public education, with potential increases in support for charter and private schools. Changes in funding may impact the resources available to public schools, especially those serving under-resourced communities. Understandably, this can create worry for families who rely on public schools as the primary source of education for their children.

Silver Lining: Growing Importance of Community and Local Support for Education

When public school funding is impacted, communities can step in to help fill the gaps. Many communities have rallied to provide school supplies, funding for extracurricular programs, and volunteer support in classrooms, making a difference even when resources are limited. If your local school faces cuts in resources, consider joining or starting a community-led initiative to support it. This could be as simple as organizing a school supply drive, volunteering as a mentor, or helping with after-school programs.

Supporting your local public schools not only provides critical assistance but also builds a stronger connection between schools and the community. Parents, neighbors, and local businesses can come together to support students, creating a network of resilience and ensuring that students continue to receive valuable learning experiences.

Chapter 7: Social Policies — Building Allyship and Inclusive Communities

Social policies impact fundamental rights, access to resources, and the protections that individuals and communities rely on for well-being and inclusion. With Donald Trump's administration, there may be potential changes to social policies affecting civil rights, social services, and protections for vulnerable populations, including LGBTQ+ individuals, racial minorities, and low-income communities. These shifts can create feelings of frustration or concern, especially for those committed to values of equality and justice.

Despite the challenges these policies may bring, this chapter explores how to turn concern into constructive allyship and advocacy. By focusing on inclusivity, supporting marginalized groups, and creating spaces where all individuals feel valued, you can make a positive impact. In times of social change, standing together in allyship becomes a powerful way to reinforce community bonds and promote justice.

Analyzing Policy: Potential Changes to Civil Rights Protections

One possible direction of Trump's administration might include shifts in civil rights protections, which could impact access to equal treatment under the law for marginalized communities. Whether these policies affect voting rights, workplace protections, or anti-discrimination laws, they can create significant obstacles for those directly impacted.

Silver Lining: Strengthening Allyship and Community Support Networks

If certain civil rights protections are scaled back, it's an opportunity to step up as an ally and provide support. Allyship means actively listening, learning, and advocating for the rights and well-being of others, especially those who may be disproportionately affected by policy changes. Look for ways to support organizations that focus on civil rights, whether through donations, volunteer work, or amplifying their messages on social media.

Consider attending workshops or training sessions on allyship, social justice, or anti-racism. These programs provide tools and insights on how to be a better ally and create inclusive spaces in your community. By taking proactive steps to support civil rights, you're helping to create a society that values equality, justice, and respect for everyone.

Analyzing Policy: Social Services and Safety Nets

Under Trump's administration, there may be adjustments to social services and safety net programs, which provide essential support for low-income families, seniors, and individuals with disabilities. While these changes can create stress for those who rely on these services, they also present opportunities for communities to step in and provide support through alternative resources.

Silver Lining: Fostering Mutual Aid and Local Support Networks

Mutual aid is a powerful way for communities to come together and support one another. By organizing or participating in mutual aid groups, you can help provide resources for those affected by reductions in social services. Mutual aid groups often offer essentials like food, clothing, and financial assistance on a community level, creating a sense of solidarity and shared responsibility.

Consider connecting with local food banks, shelters, or community centers to see how you can contribute, whether through donations or volunteer work. These efforts can help bridge the gap when social services fall short, allowing communities to support one another directly and effectively. Additionally, mutual aid networks foster a sense of unity and resilience, reinforcing that no one has to face challenges alone.

Analyzing Policy: LGBTQ+ Rights and Protections

Potential changes to policies affecting LGBTQ+ rights may include shifts in workplace protections, healthcare access, or public accommodations. For LGBTQ+ individuals and their allies, these changes can feel deeply personal and challenging. However, they also open avenues for strengthening community connections and advocating for inclusive environments.

Silver Lining: Supporting LGBTQ+ Organizations and Safe Spaces

If policies impacting LGBTQ+ rights become more restrictive, consider becoming involved with LGBTQ+ organizations, community centers, or advocacy groups. These groups often provide resources, safe spaces, and community support, creating a network of protection and empowerment for LGBTQ+ individuals.

You can also contribute to creating safe spaces in your own life—whether at work, in social circles, or online—by being a visible ally. This might mean displaying inclusive symbols, using affirming language, or standing up against discrimination. Simple acts of support signal to LGBTQ+ individuals that they are valued and respected, even when policies may not fully reflect those values.

Analyzing Policy: Protections for Immigrant and Refugee Communities

Potential shifts in immigration policies may also affect social services and protections for immigrant and refugee communities. Reduced support in these areas can create significant challenges for those navigating life in a new country. However, it's also an opportunity for allies to support immigrant communities by promoting inclusion and providing resources.

Silver Lining: Building Cultural Awareness and Supporting Immigrant Rights

Consider volunteering with immigrant and refugee support organizations in your area. These groups often need help with services like language tutoring, job placement assistance, or legal support, all of which contribute to making life easier for immigrants and refugees. By offering your time or resources, you help foster a welcoming environment and provide essential support.

Additionally, learning about the experiences of immigrant and refugee communities promotes cultural awareness and empathy. Engaging in open, respectful conversations about these topics helps build understanding and dismantles stereotypes. By supporting and learning from immigrant communities, you contribute to a more inclusive society that values diversity.

Embracing Allyship as a Form of Empowerment

Social policies may change, but your commitment to allyship, compassion, and inclusion can remain a constant source of strength. By standing with marginalized groups, advocating for justice, and promoting inclusivity, you're making a meaningful impact that uplifts everyone.

Taking action as an ally not only benefits the people you support but also reinforces your own sense of purpose and values. You'll find strength in knowing that you're contributing to a world rooted in respect and compassion, regardless of shifting policies. By connecting with others who share your commitment to allyship, you become part of a community dedicated to making a positive difference.

In times of social change, allyship is a reminder that together, we can build inclusive, resilient communities. Your actions, however small they may feel, are part of a greater movement toward justice and belonging for all.

Chapter 8: Foreign Relations — Empowering Global Awareness and Cultural Connections

Foreign policy shifts can affect everything from international trade and diplomacy to humanitarian aid and global cooperation on issues like climate change. Under Donald Trump's administration, there may be a renewed focus on "America First" principles, which could mean reduced international engagement or a more isolationist approach. For those who value global cooperation and interconnectedness, this can feel disheartening.

However, even as national policies may shift, there are ways to foster global awareness and contribute to positive international connections on a personal level. This chapter explores potential changes in foreign policy and suggests ways to build cultural understanding, support humanitarian efforts, and stay connected to the broader world.

Analyzing Policy: Emphasis on Isolationism and Nationalism

An "America First" approach might lead to policies that prioritize domestic concerns over international cooperation. This could include reduced involvement in international organizations, trade agreements, or collaborative environmental efforts. While these shifts may align with a focus on national interests, they can also limit opportunities for global problem-solving and mutual support.

Silver Lining: Cultivating Personal Global Awareness and Connections

While national policy may prioritize a more isolated stance, you have the power to foster global awareness on a personal level. Engaging with global issues, learning about different cultures, and following international news can help you stay informed and connected. Expanding your knowledge of the world not only broadens your perspective but also strengthens your understanding of shared global challenges.

Consider exploring resources that focus on world affairs and cultural exchanges, such as books, documentaries, and podcasts. You can also connect with people from other countries online or in local cultural organizations, which helps maintain a sense of global solidarity and understanding, even if policies may encourage a more inward focus.

Analyzing Policy: Changes in International Trade Agreements

Changes in trade policy could lead to shifts in economic partnerships and the availability of goods and services, potentially affecting prices and trade relationships. This focus on domestic production might be intended to stimulate the U.S. economy, but it can also create uncertainty in international economic relations.

Silver Lining: Supporting Fair Trade and Local-Global Connections

If there's a shift toward domestic production, this could be an opportunity to support fair-trade initiatives and ethical sourcing for the goods you buy. By choosing fair-trade products or items from companies that support ethical labor practices abroad, you're promoting responsible global commerce.

Supporting local businesses that engage in ethical trade or sustainable practices creates a local-global connection, allowing you to enjoy quality products while knowing your purchases make a positive impact. Many fair-trade products—such as coffee, chocolate, and textiles—come from countries where ethical purchasing directly benefits communities. By being a conscious consumer, you're fostering positive economic ties and supporting global development.

Analyzing Policy: Reduced Engagement in Global Humanitarian Efforts

A more national-focused foreign policy could result in reduced contributions to global humanitarian efforts or international aid, impacting vulnerable populations worldwide. While these shifts may aim to conserve resources domestically, they also highlight the importance of individual and community-driven humanitarian efforts.

Silver Lining: Supporting Humanitarian Organizations and Global Nonprofits

If national support for humanitarian aid is reduced, consider contributing to international nonprofits and relief organizations that provide essential resources to those in need. Many humanitarian organizations depend on donations from individuals to continue their work, offering food, water, healthcare, and education to underserved populations around the world.

You can support these efforts financially or by volunteering your time with local organizations that have international branches, such as Doctors Without Borders, the Red Cross, or UNICEF. This is a powerful way to remain engaged with global causes and provide help where it's most needed. Your involvement demonstrates that compassion and assistance can transcend borders, reinforcing a commitment to humanity regardless of policy changes.

Analyzing Policy: Changes to Climate and Environmental Agreements

If the administration reduces participation in global climate agreements, this could affect international cooperation on climate change, environmental sustainability, and conservation. For those concerned about the environment, such a shift may feel like a step backward in addressing urgent ecological challenges.

Silver Lining: Participating in Global Climate Advocacy and Environmental Actions

Even if the U.S. steps back from certain climate agreements, there are many ways for individuals to support environmental efforts on a global scale. Participate in local and international climate initiatives, advocate for sustainable practices, and connect with organizations focused on environmental conservation. For instance, you can join global campaigns like Earth Hour, participate in climate marches, or support reforestation projects.

Additionally, adopting sustainable practices in your own life contributes to global environmental health. Small actions, like reducing waste, conserving water, and supporting eco-friendly brands, add up when practiced by people worldwide. By promoting sustainability within your community and joining international environmental groups, you're taking meaningful steps to protect the planet.

Embracing Global Awareness as a Form of Empowerment

Foreign policy may shift toward isolation, but your commitment to global awareness, empathy, and connection remains a powerful influence. By fostering cultural understanding, supporting humanitarian causes, and engaging with international issues, you're contributing to a world that values cooperation and empathy.

Through small yet impactful actions, you're reinforcing a personal connection to the global community. In times when foreign policy may feel restrictive, these efforts remind you that you're part of something greater—a world bound by shared challenges, mutual understanding, and collective resilience.

When you embrace global awareness, you empower yourself to act with compassion and responsibility, regardless of political landscapes. Your efforts to stay connected, informed, and engaged contribute to a more interconnected world, one where every individual can make a positive impact.

Chapter 9: Finding Your Safe Space and Protecting Your Well-Being

When navigating political landscapes that may feel overwhelming, finding your own safe space can be incredibly grounding. A safe space is more than just a physical place; it's a mental and emotional refuge where you can recharge, process your thoughts, and focus on what brings you peace and purpose. As political changes take shape, creating a safe space for yourself is a powerful way to maintain balance and stay connected to what truly matters to you.

This chapter explores what a safe space can look like, why it's essential for your well-being, and how to build one that feels right for you. By setting intentional boundaries, nurturing positive habits, and surrounding yourself with supportive people, you can protect your mental health and build resilience, regardless of external challenges.

Recognizing the Power of Your Own Choices

In a world that can sometimes feel beyond your control, it's reassuring to remember that you always have control over your choices. The news, social media, and even daily conversations can often add stress, but by choosing how and when you engage with these influences, you create a buffer that helps protect your peace of mind.

Creating a safe space involves identifying what supports your well-being and taking steps to integrate those elements into your daily life. For some, it might mean setting aside a quiet room or corner of the home dedicated to relaxation and reflection. For others, it's about curating a digital space that includes only positive, reliable information and uplifting connections.

Your choices in this regard empower you to set boundaries that protect your mental and emotional health, helping you create an environment where you can relax, recharge, and feel safe.

Defining a "Safe Space" in Everyday Life

A safe space doesn't have to be a single, isolated place—it can be a combination of activities, environments, and routines that support your sense of well-being. Here are a few examples of what a safe space might look like:

- **Physical Space**: Create a dedicated area in your home where you can unwind. This could be a comfortable chair by a window, a cozy corner with your favorite books, or a room filled with plants and calming colors. Use this space as a place to disconnect and focus on relaxation.
- **Digital Space**: Curate a digital "safe space" by managing your social media feeds and news sources. Follow pages or accounts that inspire you, uplift you, and share positive

or informative content. Limit time on platforms or news sites that tend to increase stress or anxiety.
- **Social Space**: Build a supportive network of friends, family members, and like-minded individuals who understand your values and offer encouragement. Reach out to people who help you feel grounded and validated, especially when political or social issues feel overwhelming.

Your safe space can be a blend of all these elements, creating an environment—physical, digital, and social—that centers you and helps you manage external stressors.

Setting Healthy Boundaries with Social Media and News

While staying informed is important, constant exposure to political news and social media can be exhausting. To protect your mental health, set boundaries around your media consumption. Here are a few strategies to help:

- **Limit Time on News and Social Media**: Decide how much time you'll spend each day on news sites or social media, and set a timer if necessary. Designate specific times, like the morning or evening, for checking the news, so it doesn't dominate your day.
- **Unfollow or Mute Accounts**: Curate your social media feeds by unfollowing or muting accounts that tend to share negative or distressing content. Instead, follow pages that promote positivity, mental wellness, and topics that align with your values.
- **Take Breaks**: Periodically, take a break from the news or social media altogether. A digital detox, even if only for a day, can be refreshing and help you return with a clearer, calmer perspective.

Setting boundaries isn't about avoiding reality; it's about giving yourself the time and space to process information in a way that feels manageable.

Embracing Activities That Support Mental Health

When life feels overwhelming, grounding yourself in healthy activities can be a powerful way to reset and recharge. Consider engaging in hobbies or routines that bring you joy, help reduce stress, and contribute to your overall well-being:

- **Physical Activities**: Exercise is a great way to manage stress, as it releases endorphins that can improve your mood. Simple activities like walking, jogging, or yoga can make a difference. If you prefer something calming, try stretching or breathing exercises to help center yourself.
- **Creative Outlets**: Creative activities like drawing, painting, or coloring can be deeply therapeutic, giving you a sense of calm and accomplishment. Even adult coloring books or creative journaling can help you unwind and process your thoughts.

- **Time with Pets**: Spending time with a pet can be incredibly soothing. If you don't have a pet, consider volunteering at an animal shelter or pet-sitting. Some people even find joy in naming their pets after inspirational figures—maybe call a new pet "Harris" or "Obama" as a reminder of hope and resilience!
- **Volunteering**: Giving back to your community can be incredibly fulfilling. Volunteering for causes like anti-racism, LGBTQ+ rights, or environmental advocacy can help you feel connected to a greater purpose, providing a sense of empowerment and positivity.

Engaging in activities that bring you joy and fulfillment reinforces your resilience. These small, positive actions are like building blocks for your mental well-being, helping you stay grounded and focused.

Building a Support Network for Difficult Times

One of the most valuable components of your safe space is the network of people you surround yourself with. Having a support network gives you a space to share your experiences, express your concerns, and receive encouragement from people who understand your perspective.

Consider joining online or local support groups related to your interests or values. Many communities have groups for people who share similar beliefs or experiences, whether focused on mental wellness, political advocacy, or specific hobbies. By connecting with like-minded individuals, you create a source of strength and resilience that helps you navigate difficult times.

If you're feeling especially overwhelmed, seeking support from a mental health professional can be invaluable. Therapists and counselors provide a safe, confidential space where you can work through your feelings and develop healthy coping strategies.

Why a Safe Space Supports Long-Term Well-Being

Creating and maintaining a safe space supports not only your immediate well-being but also your long-term resilience. By protecting your peace and engaging in positive, supportive routines, you're building a foundation that helps you face challenges with strength and calm.

When you prioritize your well-being, you're better equipped to handle stress and uncertainty. This doesn't mean ignoring difficult realities but rather giving yourself the tools to process them in a healthy way. Your safe space is a reminder that no matter what's happening in the world, you have the power to protect your mental health, connect with supportive people, and find activities that nourish your spirit.

As you continue building your safe space, remember that it's a dynamic, personal space that can evolve with you. Adjust your routines, add new elements, and let it grow to meet your needs. With this foundation, you can approach life's challenges with resilience and clarity, knowing that you have a space where you're always safe, supported, and grounded.

Chapter 10: Cultivating Trusted Sources of Information and Avoiding Negativity

Staying informed is essential, but in today's media-saturated world, not all information sources are created equal. Some news outlets and social media accounts can be sources of valuable insights, while others can increase stress, confusion, or even misinformation. As you navigate changes in the political landscape, cultivating a habit of finding trusted, balanced sources of information will empower you to stay informed without becoming overwhelmed.

In this chapter, we'll explore how to identify reliable news, avoid negative influences, and engage thoughtfully with the information you consume. By setting boundaries around media and practicing discernment, you can protect your mental health while staying connected to what matters most.

Identifying Reliable News Sources

Reliable information is the foundation of a well-informed perspective. To stay grounded in reality, focus on news sources known for balanced reporting, journalistic integrity, and accountability. Here are a few tips for finding and trusting reliable information:

- **Choose Reputable News Outlets**: Look for well-established news outlets with a reputation for accurate reporting, such as major newspapers, public broadcasting services, and respected online publications. These sources generally have standards for fact-checking and journalistic ethics.
- **Seek Out Multiple Perspectives**: Sometimes, it's beneficial to read from a variety of reputable sources to gain a balanced view of an issue. Comparing reports on the same topic from different publications can help you recognize bias and ensure you're getting a fuller picture.
- **Check for Citations and Credible Sources**: Reliable news articles will often include quotes from experts, links to studies, or references to primary sources. If an article lacks credible citations, it may be an indication to question its reliability.
- **Limit Time Spent on Breaking News**: Breaking news often lacks the full context, as information is still unfolding. If an issue is still developing, try to wait for follow-up articles or updates, which usually provide a more complete and accurate picture.

By choosing reliable sources, you create a filter that allows only well-founded information into your mental space, protecting you from unnecessary stress or misinformation.

Avoiding Negative or Sensationalist Sources

Sensationalist media often prioritizes clicks over accuracy, using dramatic headlines or provocative images to attract attention. While it may be tempting to read shocking stories, these sources can elevate anxiety and foster negative emotions. Here are strategies for recognizing and avoiding sensationalism:

- **Watch Out for Emotional Headlines**: Sensationalist media often uses emotional or inflammatory language in headlines to provoke a strong reaction. Headlines that are overly negative, alarmist, or extreme are often a sign that the content is meant to elicit a response rather than provide accurate information.
- **Avoid Outlets That Rely on Opinions Over Facts**: Some news sources focus heavily on opinion pieces rather than fact-based reporting. While opinions can offer valuable insights, they should be balanced with factual information to ensure you're getting a clear view of the topic.
- **Mute or Unfollow Negative Social Media Accounts**: Social media can quickly become a source of negativity if your feed is filled with emotionally charged or divisive content. Curate your feed by muting, unfollowing, or blocking accounts that frequently share content that feels draining or distressing.
- **Limit Clickbait Content**: Clickbait articles often lack substance and are designed to keep you scrolling rather than informing you. If a headline sounds too good (or bad) to be true, it likely is. Focus on sources that prioritize quality over quantity.

By reducing exposure to negative sources, you're protecting your emotional energy and focusing on information that adds value to your understanding of the world.

Practicing Mindful Media Consumption

Mindful media consumption involves setting intentional boundaries on how and when you engage with information. This practice keeps you in control of your media environment, helping you stay informed without feeling overwhelmed. Here are a few ways to engage mindfully with news and social media:

- **Set a News Schedule**: Decide on specific times during the day to check the news, such as in the morning and evening. Avoid constantly refreshing news apps or checking for updates, as this can make you feel tethered to the news cycle and amplify stress.
- **Use News Aggregators Wisely**: If you like using apps or sites that aggregate news, customize them to show topics and sources that align with your interests and values. This way, you're more likely to see content that informs you without bombarding you with negativity.
- **Take Breaks When Needed**: Don't hesitate to take breaks from the news if you're feeling overwhelmed. Step away for a day or even a week—doing so doesn't mean you're uninformed; it means you're prioritizing your mental health. You can always catch up once you're feeling recharged.

- **Engage With Trusted Sources for Political Updates**: When a political story is particularly significant, turn to the sources you trust most. Checking in with reliable outlets prevents you from being pulled into the swirl of speculation that can often accompany political news.

Mindful media consumption reinforces your ability to choose what information you allow into your mental space, helping you avoid burnout and stay grounded.

Finding Positivity and Uplifting Content

While it's important to stay informed, balancing serious news with uplifting content can help boost your mood and remind you of the good in the world. Here's how to integrate positivity into your media routine:

- **Follow Inspirational Accounts**: Curate a list of social media accounts that share uplifting or inspiring content. Many accounts focus on topics like art, travel, history, or personal growth, offering a welcome break from hard news.
- **Subscribe to Positive News Sources**: Some media outlets focus exclusively on positive stories, such as acts of kindness, environmental successes, or community achievements. Adding a positive news site to your reading list gives you a boost of optimism.
- **Enjoy Lighthearted Content**: Take time to enjoy media that's purely for entertainment or relaxation, like comedy shows, DIY videos, or nature documentaries. These help you unwind and add a sense of balance to your day.

Balancing hard news with positive content helps you maintain a sense of well-being, even when certain topics may be stressful.

Recognizing Why Balanced Information Supports Mental Health

When you make a habit of consuming balanced, reliable information, you're not only staying informed—you're also creating a more grounded, centered perspective. Balanced media consumption provides the context and clarity needed to understand issues without feeling overwhelmed. This approach empowers you to approach information with discernment, giving you the tools to recognize bias, avoid sensationalism, and find meaning in what you read.

Knowing that you're informed in a healthy, measured way can reduce anxiety and help you feel more in control, regardless of the news itself. This balance contributes to a resilient mindset, allowing you to approach the world with clarity, curiosity, and calm.

By being intentional about the information you consume, you're creating an information "safe space" that supports your well-being. Through careful media choices, you'll find it easier to remain positive, purposeful, and empowered in times of change.

Chapter 11: Exploring Healthy Hobbies and Positive Outlets

Engaging in healthy hobbies and finding positive outlets for your energy can be one of the most rewarding ways to maintain resilience and joy, especially during challenging times. Hobbies allow you to disconnect from stressors, focus on personal growth, and reconnect with what brings you peace and happiness. When life feels overwhelming, immersing yourself in a fulfilling activity provides a necessary escape, helping you reset your mind and feel re-energized.

This chapter explores various hobbies and activities that support mental health, encourage creativity, and foster a sense of well-being. By exploring new interests and dedicating time to what you love, you're giving yourself the tools to navigate life's changes with balance and positivity.

The Benefits of Physical Activity for Stress Relief

Physical activities are well-known for their mental health benefits. Exercise releases endorphins, which improve your mood and reduce stress, making it one of the most effective ways to care for both your mind and body. Engaging in physical activity doesn't have to mean intense workouts—anything that gets you moving can help, including:

- **Walking or Jogging**: Going for a walk or jog outdoors allows you to enjoy nature, clear your mind, and get some fresh air. Even a short daily walk can improve your mood and help you feel more grounded.
- **Yoga and Stretching**: Yoga offers both physical and mental benefits, helping you to relax, improve flexibility, and focus on mindfulness. If you're new to yoga, consider trying beginner online classes or short stretching routines.
- **Dancing**: Dancing to your favorite music is a fun and uplifting way to exercise. It's a great option for those who prefer movement that doesn't feel like a traditional workout—plus, you can do it right at home.

Physical activity supports mental resilience, making you feel more capable of handling daily stressors. Finding a form of movement you enjoy turns exercise into a pleasurable, mood-boosting habit rather than a chore.

Creative Outlets for Emotional Expression

Creative activities are a wonderful way to express emotions, process thoughts, and enjoy a break from the usual routine. When you're focused on creating something, whether it's a painting, a poem, or a piece of music, you can temporarily let go of stress and tap into your imagination. Here are some creative hobbies to explore:

- **Art and Coloring**: Drawing, painting, or even using adult coloring books can be incredibly calming and meditative. Art allows you to express yourself visually, which can be therapeutic, especially if it's difficult to put your feelings into words.
- **Writing and Journaling**: Journaling is a great way to process thoughts, set goals, and reflect on your day. Try starting a gratitude journal to focus on positive aspects of your life, or explore creative writing if you enjoy storytelling. Writing helps clarify your thoughts and can serve as a release for emotions.
- **Crafting**: Knitting, crocheting, woodworking, or making jewelry are hands-on hobbies that focus your attention and provide a sense of accomplishment. Crafting something tangible can boost your mood, reduce anxiety, and help you feel productive.

Creative outlets give you a chance to step outside of yourself, experiment, and make something new. These hobbies provide a gentle and enjoyable way to channel energy into positive, constructive activities.

The Joy of Pets and Animal Companionship

Spending time with animals can bring an immense sense of calm and happiness. Pets offer unconditional companionship, making them wonderful sources of comfort during stressful times. If you don't currently have a pet, consider volunteering at a local animal shelter or pet-sitting for a friend. Here are some ways animals can add positivity to your life:

- **Caring for a Pet**: Dogs, cats, or even smaller pets like rabbits or birds can become beloved companions that bring joy and companionship to your daily life. Pets encourage routines, like regular walks or feeding times, which can be grounding and add structure to your day.
- **Volunteering at Animal Shelters**: Many shelters welcome volunteers to help with animal care, socialization, and cleaning. Spending time with animals in need not only provides comfort to the animals but also gives you a sense of purpose and community.
- **Naming and Bonding**: For some, giving a pet a special name like "Harris" or "Obama" can add an extra layer of meaning and positivity to your bond. It's a playful way to remind yourself of resilience, hope, and qualities that inspire you.

Animals can provide a sense of companionship and non-judgmental support, creating an emotional bond that promotes well-being and happiness.

Volunteering for Causes You Believe In

If you're passionate about social causes, volunteering is a fulfilling way to connect with like-minded people and make a positive difference. Whether you care about environmental protection, anti-racism, LGBTQ+ rights, or immigration advocacy, dedicating your time to these causes creates a sense of purpose and community.

- **Local Volunteer Groups**: Many communities have local organizations focused on social causes. Research volunteer opportunities in your area, whether it's helping at a food bank, cleaning up a park, or mentoring students.
- **Online Advocacy and Support**: If you're unable to volunteer in person, consider supporting causes online. Many organizations rely on social media support, petitions, and virtual events to spread awareness and advocate for change.
- **Personal Growth Through Service**: Volunteering not only benefits the community but also gives you a sense of accomplishment and purpose. By supporting causes that align with your values, you feel empowered and connected to something greater than yourself.

Volunteering provides a meaningful outlet for passion and advocacy, transforming concerns into concrete actions that make a difference.

Learning New Skills and Hobbies

Learning something new is a fantastic way to stay mentally active, boost self-esteem, and open yourself to new experiences. Whether you've always wanted to learn a language, play an instrument, or master a craft, now could be a perfect time to explore a new hobby or skill. Here are some ideas to inspire you:

- **Language Learning**: Apps like Duolingo or Rosetta Stone make learning a new language accessible and fun. Language skills are useful and can help you connect with people from different backgrounds.
- **Music and Instruments**: If you've ever wanted to play an instrument, consider starting with something simple, like the guitar, keyboard, or ukulele. Music can be therapeutic, and learning an instrument provides a creative outlet.
- **Cooking and Baking**: Trying out new recipes or perfecting a favorite dish can be relaxing and rewarding. Cooking allows you to experiment with flavors, be creative, and take pride in what you make.

Engaging in lifelong learning keeps your mind sharp, builds confidence, and gives you goals to look forward to, helping you remain positive and motivated.

Why Hobbies and Positive Outlets Support Mental Health

Hobbies give you something to look forward to each day, providing a sense of accomplishment, joy, and balance in your life. They act as anchors, grounding you in routines and activities that nurture mental well-being. When you immerse yourself in activities that bring happiness, you're creating a mental "safe space," where you can focus on personal growth and positive experiences.

Having positive outlets also helps manage stress by directing your energy into creative or physical activities, reducing anxiety and promoting relaxation. These hobbies become tools for building resilience, helping you approach life with a clear mind and a full heart.

Remember, your hobbies are a personal refuge. Allow yourself to explore what brings you joy, and take comfort in knowing that these activities are always there to support and uplift you. Through hobbies and positive outlets, you're cultivating a lifestyle that emphasizes well-being, curiosity, and the importance of self-care.

Chapter 12: Building a Support Network for Difficult Times

When navigating uncertainty or stress, having a strong support network can be one of the most valuable resources for your well-being. A support network provides you with a community cf people who understand, encourage, and stand by you during challenging moments. This group can include family, friends, colleagues, mentors, or members of support groups. By intentionally building and nurturing these connections, you create a foundation of strength that helps you feel less alone and more empowered.

In this chapter, we'll explore how to build a supportive community, reach out for help, and be there for others. Whether in person or online, cultivating meaningful connections offers a powerful source of comfort, encouragement, and resilience.

The Power of Social Connection

Humans are naturally social beings, and connecting with others offers mental and emotional benefits that are essential for well-being. Social connections reduce feelings of isolation, increase feelings of belonging, and provide a space to share experiences, hopes, and challenges. During difficult times, knowing that you have people who care about you can be deeply comforting.

Support networks provide different types of support, including:

- **Emotional Support**: Friends and family members who listen, empathize, and offer comfort during difficult times.
- **Informational Support**: Mentors, colleagues, or professionals who provide guidance and information to help you navigate challenges.
- **Instrumental Support**: Practical assistance, such as helping with tasks, providing resources, or offering transportation when needed.

By recognizing the unique strengths of each connection in your network, you can build a circle that provides comprehensive support, tailored to your needs.

Reaching Out and Asking for Help

Asking for help can feel challenging, especially if you're used to managing things on your own. However, reaching out is a sign of strength, not weakness. Sharing your experiences with others allows them to understand what you're going through, offering you their support in return.

Here are some ways to reach out for support when you need it:

- **Be Open and Honest**: When you're feeling overwhelmed, be honest with your friends or family members. Express how you're feeling and let them know how they can help, whether it's listening, providing advice, or simply spending time with you.
- **Join a Support Group**: Support groups, whether in-person or online, are spaces where you can connect with others going through similar experiences. These groups provide a safe environment to share, listen, and gain insight from people who understand what you're dealing with.
- **Seek Professional Help**: Mental health professionals, such as therapists or counselors, offer expert guidance for navigating difficult times. If you're facing challenges that feel too overwhelming to manage alone, consider seeking help from a trusted professional.

Reaching out for support strengthens your connections with others and shows that you're not alone. It's a reminder that people care about you and want to help you through life's ups and downs.

Building a Network of Like-Minded People

Surrounding yourself with people who share similar values, interests, or experiences helps create a sense of belonging. Whether you're passionate about a cause, interested in a hobby, or facing a unique life challenge, finding a community of like-minded individuals can offer invaluable camaraderie and support. Here are ways to find and connect with such groups:

- **Interest-Based Groups**: Look for local or online groups centered around your hobbies, passions, or causes you care about. Whether it's a book club, environmental organization, or crafting group, joining these communities allows you to bond over shared interests.
- **Volunteer Organizations**: Volunteering for causes like environmental conservation, social justice, or animal welfare is a great way to meet people with similar values. Working together toward a common goal fosters strong connections and a sense of shared purpose.
- **Support Communities Online**: Many online forums, social media groups, and platforms offer communities based on shared experiences or challenges. From parenting forums to chronic illness support groups, you can find spaces where people understand and share your journey.

Connecting with like-minded people offers you a support network that is both empathetic and aligned with your values. These connections provide encouragement, companionship, and often lasting friendships.

Supporting Others as Part of Your Network

Building a support network isn't just about receiving support; it's also about being there for others. Providing encouragement, listening, and offering practical help when needed strengthens relationships and creates a sense of mutual trust and respect. Supporting others can be as simple as sending a thoughtful message, offering advice, or being present when someone needs to talk.

Here are some ways to offer support to others in your network:

- **Practice Active Listening**: When a friend or family member reaches out, focus on listening without interrupting or offering solutions unless they ask. Sometimes, people just need someone to listen and empathize.
- **Check In Regularly**: Regular check-ins show that you care and are available to help. Even a quick message or call to say hello can mean a lot, especially during difficult times.
- **Celebrate Their Wins**: Support isn't only for hard times—celebrating achievements, big or small, is equally important. Recognizing and celebrating each other's accomplishments strengthens bonds and spreads positivity.

When you offer support to others, you're contributing to a cycle of kindness, resilience, and connection. This mutual exchange builds a strong, healthy network where everyone feels valued and supported.

Finding Online Communities for Additional Support

For many, online communities provide a convenient and accessible way to find support. Digital platforms offer a wide range of support groups, discussion boards, and social networks tailored to specific interests or challenges. Whether you're looking for a support group related to mental health, political advocacy, or shared hobbies, there's likely an online community that meets your needs.

Some options for finding online support include:

- **Social Media Groups**: Platforms like Facebook have groups on nearly every topic imaginable, allowing you to connect with people who share your interests or experiences.
- **Forums and Discussion Boards**: Websites like Reddit and specialized forums provide anonymous spaces where people discuss topics ranging from hobbies to health challenges. These platforms allow you to share and seek advice from others with similar experiences.
- **Mental Health Apps and Resources**: Some mental health apps offer community support features, such as forums or group therapy sessions. Examples include BetterHelp, 7 Cups, and Talkspace, which connect people for emotional support and advice.

Online communities make support accessible from anywhere, providing a safe space to share, listen, and gain insight from a diverse range of perspectives.

Why a Strong Support Network Enhances Well-Being

Having a support network gives you a foundation of understanding, empathy, and companionship that helps you handle challenges with confidence and resilience. A solid support network offers practical help, encouragement, and different perspectives, enriching your life and reminding you that you're not alone.

Feeling connected to others, knowing you have people to rely on, and contributing to others' lives strengthens your mental health and sense of purpose. Relationships built on trust and mutual support are invaluable during difficult times, creating a sense of safety and stability in a constantly changing world.

Your support network doesn't have to be large—it just needs to be meaningful. By nurturing these relationships and building a circle of people who understand and care for you, you're investing in your well-being, building a community, and ensuring you have people to lean on whenever you need them. In return, you're also creating a space where others know they can count on you, fostering a resilient, compassionate, and deeply connected community.

Chapter 13: Seeking Support from Health Professionals

Taking care of mental and physical health is crucial, especially during times of stress or uncertainty. While friends, family, and community can provide essential support, sometimes the challenges you face may require professional guidance. Mental health professionals, such as therapists, counselors, and doctors, offer specialized expertise to help you navigate difficult emotions, manage stress, and build coping skills. Seeking professional support is a proactive step toward protecting your well-being and ensuring that you have the tools needed to thrive.

This chapter explores the importance of professional health support, how to find the right mental health or medical professional, and what to expect from the experience. Engaging with a professional can be one of the most empowering and transformative steps you take in your journey toward mental and emotional resilience.

Understanding the Benefits of Professional Support

Mental health professionals are trained to help you address challenges that may feel overwhelming or complex. They offer an objective, non-judgmental perspective, creating a safe space where you can explore your emotions and develop healthy ways to cope. Here are some ways professional support can benefit you:

- **Guidance and Perspective**: Therapists and counselors can help you gain clarity on difficult emotions or situations, offering guidance to work through feelings in a constructive way.
- **Skill Development**: Mental health professionals can teach you coping mechanisms, mindfulness practices, and problem-solving skills that enhance resilience and empower you to manage stress more effectively.
- **Emotional Validation**: Professional support validates your experiences, helping you feel understood and seen. Having a space to openly express your feelings can be incredibly healing.
- **Long-Term Growth**: Therapy often facilitates personal growth, helping you build self-awareness, improve communication skills, and deepen your understanding of yourself.

Engaging with a health professional allows you to receive personalized support that addresses your unique needs, providing you with tools that you can use both now and in the future.

When to Consider Reaching Out to a Professional

If you're experiencing prolonged stress, anxiety, depression, or simply feel overwhelmed, reaching out to a mental health professional can be beneficial. Here are some signs that professional support might be helpful:

- **Persistent Feelings of Sadness or Anxiety**: If you're feeling consistently low or anxious, even when things are going well, it may be a sign to seek support. A professional can help identify underlying causes and develop strategies to improve your mental health.
- **Difficulty Managing Daily Life**: When daily tasks feel overwhelming, or if stress is impacting your ability to work, sleep, or socialize, a therapist or counselor can provide tools to help you cope and manage better.
- **Loss of Interest in Activities You Enjoy**: If you're finding it hard to engage with hobbies or activities that you once enjoyed, this could be a sign of depression or burnout. Therapy can help you explore these feelings and find ways to reignite your interests.
- **Major Life Changes**: Big transitions, like a job change, relocation, loss, or new family dynamics, can create emotional challenges. Professional support provides guidance as you navigate these changes.

Seeking help doesn't mean something is "wrong" with you—it's a proactive choice to prioritize your well-being and learn tools to handle life's challenges effectively.

Finding the Right Professional for You

Finding the right mental health professional is essential to building a supportive, productive relationship. Here's a guide to help you find a provider who meets your needs:

- **Research Different Types of Providers**: Therapists, counselors, psychologists, and psychiatrists all offer mental health support, but each has unique training and areas of expertise. Research the types of providers to determine which one may be best for your needs.
- **Look for Licensed Professionals**: Choose a licensed professional with the appropriate credentials, as this ensures they have the necessary training and adhere to ethical standards. Websites for organizations like the American Psychological Association (APA) or National Alliance on Mental Illness (NAMI) provide directories of licensed providers.
- **Consider Specialized Therapies**: Some professionals specialize in specific types of therapy, such as Cognitive Behavioral Therapy (CBT), Dialectical Behavior Therapy (DBT), or mindfulness-based approaches. Consider what type of therapy might resonate with you, or ask potential therapists about their approach.
- **Read Reviews or Get Recommendations**: Reviews and recommendations can provide insights into a therapist's style and approach. Many therapists also offer a free initial consultation, which allows you to determine if they're a good fit.

The process of finding the right professional may take time, but once you do, you'll have access to a relationship that can provide deep support and guidance.

What to Expect from Therapy or Counseling

Therapy is a collaborative process, and understanding what to expect can make it more comfortable. Here's a brief overview of the therapy experience:

- **Initial Assessment**: In the first session, your therapist will likely ask questions to understand your background, current challenges, and goals for therapy. This is a chance for you to share as much or as little as you feel comfortable with.
- **Building Trust**: Therapy is built on trust and confidentiality, allowing you to discuss your thoughts and feelings openly. The therapist's role is to listen without judgment, offering insights and tools to help you process your experiences.
- **Setting Goals Together**: Many therapists work with you to set goals, whether it's managing anxiety, improving relationships, or building self-confidence. Goals give structure to therapy and help you measure progress over time.
- **Coping Tools and Strategies**: Therapy sessions often involve learning specific techniques to cope with stress, manage emotions, or reframe negative thoughts. Practicing these tools outside of sessions reinforces your progress.

Therapy is a process that requires patience and commitment. As you work together, you may uncover new insights, develop greater self-awareness, and build a toolkit of skills that support long-term growth and resilience.

Exploring Alternative Forms of Support

In addition to traditional therapy, other forms of professional support can contribute to well-being. Some alternative or supplementary options include:

- **Support Groups**: Many people benefit from group therapy or peer support groups, where they can share experiences and learn from others. These groups are often led by a therapist or counselor and provide a sense of community and mutual support.
- **Online Therapy**: Virtual therapy has become increasingly popular and offers flexibility for those with busy schedules or limited access to in-person services. Many licensed therapists now provide secure online sessions, making it easy to receive support from the comfort of home.
- **Mindfulness and Meditation Programs**: Some professionals specialize in mindfulness-based approaches that teach techniques for managing stress and increasing self-awareness. Mindfulness programs can complement traditional therapy by enhancing relaxation and focus.

Exploring alternative forms of support allows you to find a combination that best suits your needs, ensuring you receive comprehensive care that aligns with your lifestyle.

Normalizing the Journey Toward Wellness

It's essential to remember that seeking support from health professionals is a normal, positive step toward well-being. Just as you would see a doctor for physical health concerns, turning to a mental health professional for emotional or psychological support is an important aspect of self-care.

Everyone experiences challenges, and having a professional by your side makes navigating them easier. By seeking help, you're showing a commitment to yourself, your growth, and your long-term resilience.

Embracing Professional Support as a Form of Empowerment

Engaging with mental health professionals is an empowering decision that reinforces your commitment to self-care and growth. Therapy isn't just about addressing immediate challenges; it's about building skills that can support you throughout your life.

Remember, seeking professional support is a courageous step that reflects strength, not weakness. You're investing in your well-being, learning strategies that empower you to handle stress, and giving yourself the tools to thrive.

As you continue on your journey, professional support becomes a vital part of your resilience toolkit, helping you approach life with clarity, confidence, and self-compassion. Embracing this support enables you to take control of your mental health, navigate challenges with grace, and build a life rooted in well-being and inner peace.

Chapter 14: Embracing Peacefulness and Nonviolence

In a world often marked by tension and conflict, choosing peace and nonviolence is a powerful act of resilience and strength. When external circumstances feel overwhelming or upsetting, it's natural to experience emotions like frustration or anger. However, responding with calmness and compassion enables you to maintain a sense of inner peace, even in challenging times. Choosing nonviolence doesn't mean ignoring difficulties; it's about facing them with mindfulness, empathy, and a commitment to positive change.

This chapter explores the principles of peacefulness and nonviolence, offering practical strategies for managing difficult emotions, practicing compassion, and creating a personal approach to nonviolent living. By embracing these values, you're cultivating an approach to life that prioritizes understanding, healing, and lasting change.

Understanding Nonviolence as a Philosophy and Practice

Nonviolence is more than just the absence of physical violence; it's a philosophy rooted in compassion, respect, and empathy. This approach encourages us to resolve conflicts peacefully, communicate with kindness, and find common ground. Nonviolence was central to leaders like Martin Luther King Jr. and Mahatma Gandhi, who advocated for change through peaceful means and inspired others to pursue justice without harm.

Embracing nonviolence in your own life means choosing to act with empathy, even when confronted with anger or frustration. It's about viewing challenges as opportunities for growth and transformation, fostering a mindset that seeks to build connections rather than division.

By adopting a nonviolent philosophy, you're empowering yourself to approach life with clarity and purpose, grounded in values that promote harmony and understanding.

Managing Difficult Emotions in a Peaceful Way

When faced with stressful or frustrating situations, it's natural to feel strong emotions. Anger, sadness, or anxiety can arise, especially in response to challenges that feel unfair or overwhelming. Managing these emotions in a peaceful way helps you stay calm and focused, allowing you to respond thoughtfully rather than react impulsively.

Here are some strategies for peaceful emotional management:

- **Practice Mindful Breathing**: Taking deep, slow breaths helps calm the nervous system and brings focus to the present moment. When you feel overwhelmed, take a few moments to breathe deeply, centering yourself before responding.

- **Pause Before Reacting**: If you're feeling angry or frustrated, give yourself time to pause and consider your response. This brief moment of reflection can help you respond from a place of clarity rather than reacting out of anger.
- **Acknowledge Your Emotions Without Judgment**: Recognizing your feelings without judgment allows you to process them in a healthy way. Remind yourself that emotions are natural and don't have to control your actions.
- **Engage in Physical Activities for Release**: Physical movement, like walking, jogging, or yoga, can help release pent-up emotions and clear your mind. Exercise channels your energy in a positive way and helps reduce stress.

By practicing peaceful emotional management, you're creating a foundation of calm and self-control that enables you to handle challenges with grace.

Practicing Compassion and Empathy in Daily Life

Nonviolence begins with compassion and empathy. When we choose to see situations from others' perspectives, it becomes easier to respond with understanding instead of judgment. Practicing compassion strengthens your relationships and promotes a more harmonious environment.

Here are ways to incorporate compassion and empathy into daily life:

- **Listen Actively**: Give others your full attention and listen to their words without interrupting or planning your response. Active listening shows respect and demonstrates that you value their perspective.
- **Seek to Understand**: When faced with disagreements, try to understand the other person's viewpoint. Asking questions like "What led you to feel this way?" or "Can you tell me more about your experience?" fosters empathy and can defuse tension.
- **Practice Self-Compassion**: Compassion starts within. Be kind to yourself, recognizing that everyone makes mistakes and faces challenges. By practicing self-compassion, you build a foundation for offering empathy to others.
- **Engage in Random Acts of Kindness**: Small gestures of kindness, like offering a smile, holding the door for someone, or sending a positive message, create a ripple effect that spreads goodwill and positivity.

Compassionate actions have a way of transforming situations and building trust. By consistently practicing empathy, you're contributing to a more understanding and supportive world.

Choosing Peaceful Activism

For those who feel called to address social or political issues, peaceful activism is a powerful way to advocate for change. Nonviolent activism means using respectful, constructive methods to raise awareness, educate others, and push for justice without causing harm.

Here are some peaceful ways to engage in activism:

- **Participate in Peaceful Protests**: Peaceful demonstrations allow you to voice your beliefs in a way that promotes unity and respect. Many impactful movements, from the Civil Rights Movement to environmental initiatives, were grounded in nonviolent protest.
- **Support Advocacy Organizations**: Contributing to organizations that align with your values is a way to support change on a larger scale. Donations, volunteering, or simply spreading the word about their work can help amplify positive efforts.
- **Engage in Letter-Writing Campaigns**: Writing letters to elected officials, companies, or community leaders is a peaceful and personal way to express your concerns and advocate for change.
- **Educate and Inspire Others**: Sharing knowledge, encouraging open conversations, and using social media to raise awareness are all powerful forms of peaceful activism. Education fosters understanding and helps others see the importance of issues you care about.

Peaceful activism empowers you to make a difference in ways that build up rather than tear down. It channels your passion for change into actions that promote respect, understanding, and unity.

Creating Personal Peace Through Daily Rituals

In addition to engaging peacefully with the world, it's essential to cultivate inner peace. Creating daily rituals that encourage calmness, reflection, and mindfulness helps you approach life with a balanced and centered mindset.

Here are a few rituals for cultivating inner peace:

- **Morning Meditation or Reflection**: Begin each day with a few minutes of meditation or quiet reflection. This practice centers your mind, helping you approach the day with clarity and calm.
- **Practice Gratitude**: Taking time to reflect on what you're grateful for can shift your mindset to positivity. Gratitude practices, such as journaling or simply listing three things you're thankful for, promote a peaceful outlook.
- **Spend Time in Nature**: Nature has a grounding effect and can help reduce stress. Whether you take a walk in a nearby park or enjoy a cup of tea by an open window, spending time in nature fosters peace and tranquility.
- **Limit Exposure to Negative Media**: Consuming news or social media with distressing content can elevate stress. Set boundaries around media consumption, choosing instead to engage with uplifting content that reinforces peace.

Rituals create a sense of stability, helping you maintain calm and focus throughout the day. By prioritizing personal peace, you build resilience and inner strength.

Why Peacefulness and Nonviolence Strengthen Resilience

Choosing peacefulness and nonviolence strengthens resilience because it enables you to handle stress without compromising your values. When you prioritize calm and compassion, you're not only creating a positive impact on others but also building a mindset that protects your mental and emotional health.

Nonviolence empowers you to approach challenges with clarity, giving you a way to face difficulties without being consumed by them. This mindset reinforces the belief that meaningful change can happen through empathy, understanding, and cooperation.

Embracing peacefulness doesn't mean avoiding action; it's about choosing intentional actions that align with your values. By committing to nonviolence, you're reinforcing a way of life that uplifts, heals, and strengthens both yourself and those around you.

Embracing Peace as a Path to Personal and Collective Well-Being

Peacefulness and nonviolence are powerful choices that transform how you interact with the world and yourself. By committing to these principles, you're nurturing a life centered on compassion, understanding, and integrity. You're building a foundation of resilience that allows you to respond thoughtfully to challenges, protect your inner peace, and contribute positively to society.

Through peaceful living, you're making a conscious choice to build bridges rather than barriers, to uplift rather than harm, and to create an environment where respect and kindness prevail. As you continue on this journey, remember that every peaceful action—no matter how small—creates ripples of positivity, helping to shape a world where peace and empathy are valued by all.

Chapter 15: Why Self-Care and Community Support Help Manage Stress

Self-care and community support are two of the most effective ways to maintain mental and emotional resilience. By nurturing yourself and connecting with a supportive community, you're building a strong foundation that helps you manage stress, navigate challenges, and thrive in the face of adversity. While self-care involves personal actions that prioritize well-being, community support provides a network of care that strengthens your sense of belonging and security.

In this final chapter, we'll explore why self-care and community support are essential for stress management, how they complement each other, and practical ways to incorporate both into your daily life. Together, these practices empower you to lead a balanced, fulfilling life, even when circumstances are uncertain.

Understanding the Importance of Self-Care for Resilience

Self-care involves actions and practices that support your physical, mental, and emotional health. When you prioritize self-care, you're ensuring that you have the energy and clarity to handle life's challenges effectively. Far from being selfish, self-care is a necessity for building resilience and maintaining well-being.

Here's how self-care helps manage stress:

- **Reduces Physical and Mental Fatigue**: Self-care practices, like adequate sleep, nutritious eating, and regular exercise, help maintain your energy levels and reduce feelings of burnout. Taking care of your physical health makes you more resilient to stress.
- **Strengthens Emotional Resilience**: Self-care activities like journaling, meditation, or hobbies allow you to process your emotions and recharge. By making time for yourself, you build emotional reserves that help you handle challenges calmly.
- **Promotes Mindfulness**: Practicing self-care helps you stay mindful and connected to the present. When you're fully engaged in self-care activities, you're taking a break from worries about the past or future, reducing anxiety.
- **Encourages Self-Compassion**: Self-care reminds you to treat yourself with kindness and patience. Practicing self-compassion enables you to forgive yourself for mistakes and approach challenges without self-judgment.

Self-care is the cornerstone of resilience. By nurturing yourself, you're strengthening your ability to cope with stress and take on life's challenges with confidence.

The Role of Community Support in Reducing Stress

Community support provides a network of care, understanding, and encouragement. When you connect with others who share similar values, interests, or experiences, you build a circle of people who uplift and support each other. Community support reduces feelings of isolation, creates a sense of shared purpose, and offers practical assistance during difficult times.

Here's why community support is vital for managing stress:

- **Creates a Sense of Belonging**: Being part of a community helps you feel connected and understood. A sense of belonging provides comfort and stability, which are essential for mental well-being.
- **Offers Emotional Support**: In times of stress, talking with others can offer relief and reassurance. Friends, family, and support groups provide a safe space to express yourself without judgment, helping to alleviate anxiety and fear.
- **Provides Practical Help**: Communities often offer practical assistance, whether it's helping with tasks, offering resources, or sharing knowledge. Knowing that you can rely on others for support when needed reduces the burden of stress.
- **Fosters Empathy and Shared Resilience**: Engaging in community support teaches you the value of empathy and encourages you to contribute to others' well-being. This sense of shared resilience reinforces the idea that you're not alone in facing life's challenges.

Community support enhances your ability to cope with stress by providing a stable, understanding network. It gives you the confidence to face difficulties with the reassurance that others are there for you.

Chapter 16: Embracing Resilience and Empowerment in Uncertain Times

As you reach the final chapter of this guide, it's time to bring together all the tools, insights, and practices you've explored. Life's challenges are inevitable, but your approach to them can make a world of difference. Resilience is not about avoiding hardship; it's about developing the strength, adaptability, and perspective to face difficulties with grace and purpose. Empowerment comes from knowing that you have control over how you respond to circumstances, that you can find meaning and growth even in adversity.

In this chapter, we'll reflect on what it means to embrace resilience and empowerment, how to maintain a positive mindset in uncertain times, and ways to continually build inner strength. By fully embracing resilience, you're choosing to live a life that is centered, adaptable, and deeply fulfilling.

Understanding Resilience as a Dynamic Process

Resilience isn't a single quality you either have or don't have—it's a dynamic process that grows and changes with you. Resilience is developed through the ways you respond to life's challenges, by learning from setbacks, and by finding the courage to continue even when the path is difficult. Each time you choose to face a hardship with strength, you're building resilience.

Here's what resilience looks like in practice:

- **Adaptability**: Life often brings the unexpected, but resilience helps you adapt without losing your sense of purpose. Being flexible in your approach allows you to find new ways forward, even when plans change.
- **Positive Reframing**: Resilient people are skilled at reframing challenges to see opportunities for growth or meaning. While difficulties may still be painful, viewing them as learning experiences adds a layer of hope and positivity.
- **Commitment to Self-Care**: Resilience requires self-care to maintain the mental and emotional energy needed to persevere. By prioritizing well-being, you're fortifying yourself against the stresses of life.
- **Seeking Support**: Resilience also involves reaching out to others when needed. Strong, resilient people recognize the value of community and know that it's okay to ask for help.

Resilience is a skill you build over time, and every challenge you overcome adds to your strength. It's a lifelong process of growth that empowers you to approach life with optimism and purpose.

Empowerment Through Self-Belief and Agency

Empowerment comes from understanding your own agency—the knowledge that you have the ability to make choices, set boundaries, and direct your life. Embracing empowerment means recognizing that, even when external circumstances are beyond your control, you have control over your actions, thoughts, and responses.

Ways to build and maintain a sense of empowerment include:

- **Setting Intentions and Goals**: Intentions and goals give you a sense of direction. By setting meaningful goals, whether short- or long-term, you're taking proactive steps to shape your future.
- **Practicing Assertiveness**: Empowerment includes the ability to assert your needs, boundaries, and beliefs with respect and confidence. Practicing assertiveness reinforces your sense of self-worth and autonomy.
- **Celebrating Small Wins**: Recognize and celebrate every step forward, no matter how small. Each success is a reminder of your strength and capabilities, reinforcing a positive sense of self.
- **Owning Your Choices**: Empowerment also comes from fully owning your decisions and actions. Knowing that you're in charge of your choices reinforces your agency and helps you feel confident in your path.

Empowerment is about believing in yourself and your potential. It's a mindset that encourages you to take ownership of your life, recognize your strengths, and approach challenges with confidence.

Cultivating a Positive Mindset in Uncertain Times

In times of uncertainty, maintaining a positive mindset can make a powerful difference. A positive mindset doesn't mean ignoring hardships or forcing yourself to be optimistic at all times; it's about cultivating hope, gratitude, and self-compassion. This mindset acts as a buffer against stress, helping you remain focused on what's within your control.

Here are some ways to cultivate positivity in challenging times:

- **Focus on What You Can Control**: Shifting your focus to aspects within your control reduces feelings of helplessness. Small actions—like setting daily routines or focusing on a meaningful hobby—help create a sense of stability.
- **Practice Gratitude Daily**: Gratitude is one of the most effective ways to boost positivity. Try listing a few things you're grateful for each day, no matter how simple. This practice helps reframe your perspective and fosters appreciation.
- **Allow Yourself to Feel**: Positivity isn't about suppressing difficult emotions; it's about making room for them without being consumed by them. Allow yourself to process

feelings of sadness, frustration, or worry, and practice self-compassion during difficult times.

- **Engage in Uplifting Activities**: Activities that bring you joy, like listening to music, watching uplifting movies, or spending time in nature, help lift your spirits and recharge your mental energy.

A positive mindset is a valuable asset, one that encourages resilience and reminds you of the good in your life, even during uncertain times.

Building Inner Strength Through Reflection and Self-Discovery

Inner strength is the foundation of resilience and empowerment. Developing inner strength involves reflecting on your experiences, learning from challenges, and discovering what truly matters to you. The more you know yourself, the more grounded you feel in the face of life's ups and downs.

Here's how to cultivate inner strength:

- **Reflect on Past Challenges**: Consider the challenges you've overcome and the strengths you used to face them. Reflecting on your past resilience reminds you of your inner resources and reinforces confidence.
- **Identify Your Core Values**: Knowing your core values gives you a sense of purpose and direction. Take time to identify the principles that guide you, whether they include kindness, integrity, growth, or compassion.
- **Practice Mindfulness and Self-Awareness**: Mindfulness helps you connect with the present moment and become aware of your thoughts, emotions, and reactions. This self-awareness builds inner strength, helping you approach life with intention and calm.
- **Embrace Growth as a Lifelong Journey**: Recognize that growth is ongoing. Embracing life as a journey of continuous learning and self-discovery helps you stay open to new experiences, making it easier to adapt and grow with each challenge.

By cultivating inner strength, you're building a sense of self that is resilient, adaptable, and ready to face whatever comes your way.

Embracing Resilience and Empowerment as a Way of Life

Resilience and empowerment are lifelong practices, ones that grow and evolve with each new experience. By choosing to embrace these qualities, you're committing to a life that values strength, self-awareness, and positive action. You're equipping yourself with the tools to not only handle difficulties but also to thrive and find fulfillment in every chapter of your life.

As you move forward, remember that resilience doesn't mean being unaffected by hardships—it means rising to meet them with a sense of purpose. Empowerment isn't about having all the answers; it's about believing in your ability to navigate the journey. Together, resilience and empowerment provide you with a compass for navigating both calm and stormy seas.

A Life Rooted in Resilience and Empowerment

Living with resilience and empowerment means taking ownership of your life, embracing each day with a sense of purpose and strength. This journey is about more than surviving; it's about flourishing, finding meaning, and making a positive impact in your own unique way.

As you close this guide, know that you have the capacity for extraordinary resilience and the power to empower yourself and others. Each choice you make, each step you take toward growth, self-care, and community, strengthens your foundation.

In embracing resilience and empowerment, you're shaping a life that is grounded, resilient, and full of potential. You have everything you need within you to face life's challenges, to support others, and to build a future rooted in strength, compassion, and boundless possibility.

Chapter 17: Finding Meaning and Purpose in Challenging Times

During uncertain and challenging periods, finding a sense of meaning and purpose can provide direction, comfort, and hope. Purpose is what gives your life focus and connects you to what you find meaningful. In difficult times, having a purpose helps you stay resilient, reminding you of why you persevere. By grounding yourself in what matters most to you, you're able to face hardships with clarity and determination.

This chapter explores ways to discover and nurture your purpose, especially when life feels complex or overwhelming. By aligning with your values, exploring your passions, and contributing to something greater than yourself, you're building a life infused with meaning and resilience.

Understanding the Power of Purpose

Purpose is a guiding force that brings intention to your actions and offers a deeper sense of fulfillment. People who feel connected to a purpose often experience greater well-being and resilience, as purpose provides motivation and a sense of belonging. Purpose can be as grand as a lifelong mission or as simple as showing kindness each day. What matters is that it resonates with you personally.

Here's how purpose can positively impact your life:

- **Enhances Resilience**: Purpose acts as a stabilizing force during challenging times, reminding you of what you're working toward and helping you keep going, even when obstacles arise.
- **Provides Motivation**: When you're connected to a purpose, daily tasks and routines feel more meaningful, helping you stay motivated and engaged.
- **Boosts Mental Health**: People with a sense of purpose report higher levels of happiness, life satisfaction, and lower stress. Purpose provides emotional support, enhancing well-being.
- **Fosters Connection with Others**: Purpose often involves relationships, whether through family, community, or shared goals. This connection reinforces a sense of belonging and unity.

Finding your purpose is a journey, and it evolves with you. Discovering what gives your life meaning opens a path to fulfillment, helping you navigate difficult times with greater focus and hope.

Exploring Your Values and Passions

Purpose is often rooted in your core values and passions. Reflecting on these can help you identify what gives you joy, motivates you, and aligns with your sense of self. By connecting with your values, you're building a foundation for purpose that is both authentic and meaningful.

Here are some ways to explore your values and passions:

- **Identify Your Core Values**: Consider what principles matter most to you, such as kindness, integrity, learning, or creativity. Write down your top values and think about how they influence your decisions and actions.
- **Reflect on Activities that Bring Joy**: Think about hobbies, activities, or subjects that spark curiosity and happiness. Passions can often point you toward a purpose that brings fulfillment.
- **Notice What Challenges Inspire You**: Sometimes, purpose arises from challenges you feel compelled to address, like social justice, environmental causes, or mental health awareness. These challenges can provide direction for meaningful action.
- **Ask Yourself Questions**: Reflect on questions like, "What do I want to contribute to the world?" or "What legacy would I like to leave behind?" These reflections can help clarify your purpose.

By aligning your purpose with your values and passions, you're creating a path that feels true to who you are, making it easier to stay committed to it.

Creating a Sense of Purpose through Contribution

Purpose often comes from contributing to something beyond yourself, whether it's a cause, a community, or even helping loved ones. When you contribute to the well-being of others, you experience a sense of fulfillment and connection that enriches your life. Acts of kindness, volunteer work, and community engagement all offer ways to live purposefully.

Ways to create purpose through contribution include:

- **Engage in Volunteering**: Volunteering connects you with causes and communities that align with your values. Whether it's working at a shelter, mentoring youth, or participating in environmental projects, volunteering gives you a chance to make a positive impact.
- **Practice Everyday Acts of Kindness**: Purpose doesn't have to involve grand gestures. Small acts of kindness, like helping a neighbor, supporting a friend, or donating to a cause, contribute to a meaningful life.
- **Support a Cause You Believe In**: Getting involved with a cause you care about can be incredibly fulfilling. Joining advocacy groups, supporting charities, or participating in local events allows you to be part of something meaningful.
- **Strengthen Family and Community Bonds**: Purpose can also come from nurturing relationships. Supporting family, building community connections, and being present for loved ones create purpose by contributing to the well-being of those around you.

When you contribute to others, you experience a sense of purpose that extends beyond personal goals, reminding you of your ability to make a difference in the lives of others.

Creating Purpose Through Personal Growth

Purpose doesn't always have to involve external causes; it can also be about personal growth and becoming the best version of yourself. Committing to self-improvement and learning brings a sense of purpose by allowing you to live up to your potential and fulfill your personal goals.

Here are ways to find purpose through personal growth:

- **Set Personal Goals**: Identify goals that resonate with you, whether it's improving your health, learning a new skill, or advancing in your career. Working toward these goals gives you direction and a sense of achievement.
- **Commit to Lifelong Learning**: Learning new things keeps life engaging and brings a sense of purpose. Whether you're learning for career advancement, personal interest, or self-discovery, lifelong learning enriches your life.
- **Focus on Inner Growth**: Personal growth includes developing qualities like compassion, patience, and resilience. When you focus on inner growth, you're committing to a purpose that benefits both yourself and those around you.
- **Set a Practice of Reflection**: Regular reflection helps you track progress, set new intentions, and stay connected to your purpose. Journaling, meditating, or simply taking time to reflect gives you a deeper understanding of your journey.

Personal growth provides a purpose that is deeply fulfilling, allowing you to continually discover and develop your strengths.

Finding Purpose in Meaningful Work and Activities

Purpose can also come from the work you do, whether it's a career, a hobby, or a side project. Engaging in meaningful activities that align with your skills and interests helps create a sense of purpose and fulfillment in daily life. Purposeful work doesn't have to be grand or world-changing; it simply needs to be meaningful to you.

Ways to create purpose through work and activities include:

- **Pursue a Career that Aligns with Your Values**: If possible, seek work that reflects your values and allows you to use your strengths. A fulfilling career provides daily purpose and a sense of accomplishment.
- **Take Up Passion Projects**: Passion projects, such as writing, art, or creating a small business, allow you to engage with activities you love. These projects bring joy and satisfaction, contributing to a sense of purpose.

- **Engage in Hobbies that Fulfill You**: Hobbies offer a space to explore interests without pressure. By engaging in hobbies you love, you're connecting with what brings you happiness and purpose.
- **Invest in Skill Development**: Developing skills that interest you, whether for work or personal growth, fosters a sense of accomplishment. Skill-building activities, like learning a new language or playing an instrument, add purpose to your free time.

Purposeful work and activities give your day structure and motivation, enriching your life and helping you feel connected to a greater sense of meaning.

Embracing Purpose as a Journey, Not a Destination

Remember that purpose is a journey, not a final destination. Your sense of purpose may evolve as you grow, face new experiences, and gain insights. Embrace this process, allowing your purpose to change as you do. Purpose is not something you "find" once and for all—it's something you create, nurture, and refine over time.

When you view purpose as a journey, you release the pressure of needing to have everything figured out. You're free to explore, try new things, and follow what feels meaningful to you in the present moment.

Living a Life of Purposeful Resilience

Living with purpose doesn't remove life's challenges, but it gives you a reason to keep going when things get tough. Purpose adds meaning to your resilience, transforming it from merely enduring difficulties to growing and learning from them. By embracing purpose, you're creating a life that feels deeply rewarding and aligned with your values.

As you move forward, remember that your purpose doesn't have to be grand or world-changing to be meaningful. Whether it's caring for family, advocating for a cause, or pursuing personal growth, your purpose is uniquely yours—and it's valuable.

In times of uncertainty, let your purpose be your anchor, guiding you through life with intention, compassion, and hope. With purpose as your foundation, you're not only building resilience—you're creating a life that reflects your deepest values and aspirations.

Chapter 18: Continuing Your Journey with Hope and Optimism

As you conclude this guide, remember that life is a continuous journey filled with both challenges and opportunities for growth. Moving forward with hope and optimism is a powerful way to navigate uncertain times and find joy, even in unexpected places. While challenges are inevitable, maintaining a hopeful outlook allows you to see possibilities, embrace change, and find meaning in each experience. Optimism doesn't ignore difficulties; instead, it gives you the strength to face them with courage and resilience.

In this final chapter, we'll reflect on the importance of hope and optimism, explore ways to cultivate a positive mindset, and consider how to carry these values with you as you continue on your journey. By choosing hope, you're setting a foundation for a fulfilling, empowered, and joyful life.

The Power of Hope in Uncertain Times

Hope is more than just wishful thinking—it's a deeply rooted belief in the possibility of positive outcomes, even when the path forward is unclear. Hope fuels perseverance, helping you find the strength to continue even when faced with setbacks. It's a powerful mindset that reminds you that things can improve and that change is always possible.

Here's why hope is essential:

- **Inspires Resilience**: Hope gives you the energy to keep going, even when challenges arise. It reinforces your resilience by helping you envision a positive future and believe in your ability to overcome obstacles.
- **Promotes Well-Being**: Studies show that people who maintain hope report higher levels of happiness and life satisfaction. Hope enhances mental and emotional well-being, reducing feelings of stress and anxiety.
- **Encourages Positive Action**: Hope often inspires constructive action. When you believe in positive possibilities, you're more likely to take steps toward achieving them, creating momentum toward change.
- **Strengthens Relationships**: Hope fosters a positive environment that encourages connection and trust. People are naturally drawn to hopeful individuals, creating a support network that uplifts everyone involved.

By choosing to cultivate hope, you're creating a mindset that supports your overall well-being and encourages you to move forward with confidence and purpose.

Cultivating Optimism as a Daily Practice

Optimism is a way of viewing the world through a positive lens, focusing on possibilities rather than limitations. While optimism doesn't deny difficulties, it emphasizes a proactive, solution-oriented approach to challenges. Cultivating optimism is a practice that requires intention and consistency, but over time, it becomes a natural way of approaching life.

Here are ways to practice optimism daily:

- **Practice Gratitude**: Focusing on what you're grateful for shifts your perspective to what's going well, reinforcing positivity. Take a moment each day to write down or reflect on three things you appreciate.
- **Reframe Challenges as Opportunities**: When you encounter obstacles, ask yourself what you can learn from them. This mindset helps you see challenges as opportunities for growth, making it easier to stay positive.
- **Use Positive Language**: The words you choose impact your mindset. Try to use encouraging language, both when talking to others and yourself. Replace negative phrases like "I can't" with "I'll try" or "I'll learn."
- **Surround Yourself with Positive Influences**: Spend time with people who inspire and uplift you. Being around optimistic individuals reinforces your own positive mindset and encourages you to see the good in every situation.
- **Visualize Positive Outcomes**: Take a few minutes each day to imagine your goals and dreams coming true. Visualization is a powerful tool that boosts optimism and motivates you to take steps toward your aspirations.

Optimism is a skill that grows with practice, helping you build resilience and approach life with a balanced, hopeful outlook.

Balancing Realism with Optimism and Hope

It's essential to recognize that optimism doesn't mean ignoring reality. A balanced perspective allows you to acknowledge challenges while still choosing to focus on positive possibilities. This balance—often called "realistic optimism"—helps you stay grounded without losing hope.

Here's how to practice realistic optimism:

- **Acknowledge Difficult Emotions**: Allow yourself to feel emotions like sadness, frustration, or fear without judgment. Embracing these feelings rather than avoiding them creates a healthy balance between hope and reality.
- **Focus on Solutions, Not Just Problems**: When you encounter challenges, focus on what you can do to improve the situation rather than dwelling on obstacles. This shift empowers you to take constructive action.
- **Set Achievable Goals**: Set realistic goals that align with your abilities and circumstances. Achieving small wins reinforces optimism, while setting overly ambitious goals can lead to disappointment.

- **Practice Self-Compassion**: Being kind to yourself is essential. Recognize that setbacks are part of life, and give yourself permission to rest, regroup, and move forward with self-compassion.

Balancing optimism with realism allows you to stay hopeful while remaining grounded. It's a perspective that helps you navigate challenges with both clarity and positivity.

Carrying Hope and Optimism with You on Your Journey

As you move forward, remember that hope and optimism are choices you can make daily. Life will bring both joy and challenges, but by choosing to see the possibilities, you're opening yourself up to new experiences and growth. Here are some ways to carry these values with you:

- **Create a Vision Board**: Vision boards are visual reminders of your hopes, dreams, and goals. Creating one can help you stay focused on what inspires you, reinforcing optimism as you work toward your aspirations.
- **Develop a Personal Affirmation**: Affirmations are positive statements that reinforce self-belief and hope. Create a personal affirmation, such as "I have the strength to overcome challenges" or "I am open to positive possibilities," and repeat it to yourself each day.
- **Celebrate Small Victories**: Take time to celebrate small achievements and progress. Recognizing these moments reinforces a hopeful mindset, reminding you that each step forward is valuable.
- **Reflect on Your Growth**: Regularly take time to reflect on how far you've come and the strengths you've developed. Acknowledging your growth helps you feel hopeful about the future and proud of your journey.
- **Stay Open to New Possibilities**: Embrace life's surprises, even when they're unexpected. Staying open to change and new experiences creates room for growth, learning, and unforeseen joys.

Carrying hope and optimism with you means choosing to live with intention, curiosity, and a belief in positive possibilities. These values create a strong foundation, empowering you to face each day with courage and resilience.

Embracing Hope and Optimism as Life-Long Companions

Hope and optimism are not just reactions to good times—they are powerful companions that guide you through both highs and lows. By embracing these values, you're choosing a life that celebrates growth, values resilience, and finds joy in each step of the journey.

As you continue forward, remember that hope and optimism are practices you can cultivate, no matter what life brings. They are rooted in your ability to see potential, believe in yourself, and trust that each experience has something to teach you. In uncertain times, hope reminds you that positive change is possible, while optimism empowers you to approach challenges with courage and creativity.

A Journey Rooted in Possibility

Choosing to live with hope and optimism is choosing a path of possibility. It's a commitment to find meaning, embrace growth, and believe in the beauty of the journey. As you carry these values forward, you're not only enriching your own life but also inspiring others to live with positivity and purpose.

Remember that you have the strength, resilience, and capacity to face whatever comes your way. Hope and optimism are your companions, guiding you toward a life that is full of potential, meaning, and joy. By embracing these values, you're creating a future that reflects the best of who you are—resilient, empowered, and open to all the wonders life has to offer.